99 Things Women Wish They Knew Before®... Dating After 40, 50, & Yes, 60!

A woman's guide to avoiding
dating disasters

Amy Sherman, LMHC &
Rosalind Sedacca, CCT

D1484228

www.99-series.com

The 99 Series
600 Brunet
Montreal, QC H4M1X8
Canada
323-203-0548

The author has done his/her best to present accurate and up-to-
date information in this book, but he/she cannot guarantee that the
information is correct or will suit your particular situation.

This book is sold with the understanding that the publisher and the
author are not engaged in rendering any legal, accounting or any
other professional services. If expert assistance is required, the
services of a competent professional should be sought.

First published by The 99 Series 2010

Ginger Marks Cover designed and Layout by
DocUmeantDesigns *www.DocUmeantDesigns.com*

Copy Edits by **the Authors Advantage**
www.theAuthorsAdvantage.com

Distributed by DocUmeant Publishing
For inquiries about volume orders, please contact:

Helen Georgaklis
99 Book Series, Inc.
600 Brunet Avenue
Montreal, Quebec
Canada
H4M 1X8

Helen@99-series.com

Printed in the United States Of America
ISBN-13: 978-0-9866629-4-2 (paperback)
ISBN-10: 0986662941

WORDS OF PRAISE

FOR…

---

99 Things You Wish You Knew Before®… ®… Dating After 40, 50, & Yes, 60!

"99 Things is filled with wisdom you never got growing up and you can't get from your friends. It's not just a good guide to dating, it's a smart guide to living." **- Judith Sherven, PhD and Jim Sniechowski, PhD, *Best-selling Authors of The Smart Couple's Guide to the Wedding of Your Dreams http://smartweddingcouples***

"As both a psychotherapist and a woman from the 'sixties set' who just returned to the dating scene I was amazed at how 'on target' this book is!! Not only were the messages those that I would deliver as a therapist, but reading them helped guide me through

this new venture in my own life...a truly helpful read!" - Mimi Scott, PhD, LCSW Author of Split: Tales from Children of Divorce

"This small book packs a really big punch, and provides solid, grounded answers to the big questions mature women often find themselves asking. I was especially impressed with 'Things' #64 to #72! Kudos to Sedacca and Sherman for providing readers with a tangible way of assessing major red flags and staying out of relationships with potential abusers! This book is a "must-buy" for all the women in your life!" - **Jackie Black, Ph.D.,** *Author of Meeting Your Match: Cracking the Code to Successful Relationships*

"This book is witty, wise and absolutely wonderful! Starting over at any age can be hard, but when you've been out of the loop for a while it's sometimes downright terrifying. These ladies have broken it down into organized and easy to read snippets that cover the gambit from sensible to sexual and everything in between. I will definitely recommend it to all of my divorcing women clients!" - **Lisa C. Decker,** *Certified Divorce Financial Analyst, www.DivorceMoneyMatters.com Miss Money Matters*™ *www.MissMoneyMatters.com*

"This is NOT another "quick fix" to dating but a foundation of how dating paradigms shift with age. Rosalind & Amy deliver a step-by-step guide that is easy to follow and can be implemented instantly! What I admire most is their ability to portray the advantages that age & experience can bring to the table! Dating at 20 was 'crazy', dating as boomers becomes dating 'smart'. Rosalind & Amy show you that creating long term, lasting relationships at this age with an emotionally available and stable partner is not only in your cards but attainable step-by-step!"
-Ben Winkler, *Relationship Coach for Singles, www.BenWinkler.com*

"99 Things is a must-read for those who are willing to create a great relationship at any age! The tips are relevant and timely, and will assist you with dating and finding love in your life." - **Krista Bloom, Ph.D., *Clinical Sexologist and author of the Ultimate Compatibility Quiz www.healingcouch.com***

"An amazing accomplishment in touching upon so many essential components regarding "Women and Dating" so concisely. If you are in therapy, use this book as a checklist. It can open the door to a lot of valuable work. If not in therapy, use it as your own pre-dating checklist in the same way a pilot would

use a pre-flight check before takeoff. Do not leave the ground without it." **-C. Paul Wanio, Ph.D., LMFT, LMHC,** *and author of, I Love You ...I Think: When Sex Disguises Itself As Love.*

DEDICATION

This book is dedicated to all the women who have struggled in relationships and all the lessons they have taught us.

CONTENTS

ABOUT THE 99 SERIES

The 99 Series is a collection of quick, easy-to-understand guides that spell it all out for you in the simplest format; 99 points, one lesson per page. The book series is the one-stop shop for all readers tired of looking all over for self-help books. The 99 Series brings it all to you under one umbrella! The bullet point format that is the basis for all the 99 Series books was created purposely for today's fast-paced society. Not only does information have to be at our finger tips… we need it quickly and accurately without having to do much research to find it. But don't be fooled by the easy-to-read format. Each of the books in the series contains very thorough discussions from our roster of professional authors so that all the information you need to know is compiled into one book!

We hope that you will enjoy this book as well as the rest of the series. If you've enjoyed our books, tell your friends. And if you feel we need to improve something, please feel free to give us your feedback at www.99-series.com.

Helen Georgaklis
Founder & CEO, 99 Series

PREFACE

Are you tired of getting into relationships that go nowhere? Fed-up with making poor choices–or wasting time on partners who don't share your 'path'? Then this is the book for you. Dating at midlife has its own special challenges. To succeed, it's important to be realistic about what you can and cannot expect from a romantic, long-term relationship.

At midlife, your purpose shifts from the superficial to the meaningful, from external gratification to internal satisfaction and purpose. Many boomer women find themselves ready to start dating again, but hesitate due to fear or other concerns. Will anyone find me desirable? Should I even try? Is it really possible to find that meaningful relationship at this stage of my life?

You are in your prime of life and have a lot of living ahead of you. So when you're looking for that special someone, realize that your partner doesn't have to be perfect. However, they have to possess certain qualities and display certain tendencies that should be the criteria upon which you base your relationship.

You know from your past history that some of your relationships have been very difficult. In most cases the challenge comes from maintaining intimacy, trust and respect for your partner. As authors of this book, we both bring more than twenty years experience in the relationship field. *Rosalind Sedacca* is a Relationship Coach and Certified Corporate Trainer. *Amy Sherman* is a Licensed Mental Health Counselor.

This book will address the key points we feel you need to know before you begin a romantic relationship. *99 Things Women Wish They Knew Before Dating After 40, 50, & YES, 60!* will empower you so that you can avoid the pitfalls and mistakes many women face and increase the likelihood of developing a healthy, mutually satisfactory bond with your significant other.

It's time that you stopped being an observer, watching and waiting and letting life go on without you. Become part of the action. Create your best life. This book will show you how to step outside your comfort zone into a place of insight, awareness and conscious decision-making. You **can** have the relationship you desire and deserve. Don't let it pass you by!

ACKNOWLEDGMENTS

We owe a debt of gratitude to Helen Georgaklis and Michael Wells for their foresight and vision in coming up with the brilliant concept of the 99 series. Also, a special thank you to Ginger Marks for her unending patience and consideration during the editing process.

We wish to thank all the women whose stories we have shared who have given us the wisdom to learn from their mistakes. We honor you all.

Amy Sherman, LMHC
Rosalind Sedacca, CCT

To our mother and my family—Robert, Nicole, Ethan and Amy—thank you for believing in me and for supporting me with your enthusiasm and love.

On a personal note, I would like to express my gratitude and love to my sister, Rosalind Sedacca, without whom this project would never have manifested. Thank you for your insights and expertise and for being such a huge source of strength and beauty.

Amy Sherman, LMHC

I want to acknowledge my mother who motivated me to really care about women and sincerely thank my husband Rick, my son Cassidy and his lovely wife Kara.

I also want to share with everyone what a blessing it is to have such a loving and supportive sister in my life—and in my heart—at all times.

Rosalind Sedacca, CCT

DATING

PREPAREDNESS QUIZ

**Test your Emotional Readiness for
Getting Back into Dating**

Use this quiz as an assessment gauge to
determine your readiness for dating. It is
designed to capture your views about starting to
date and ultimately moving into a meaningful
relationship. Use it as a tool for self-discovery.
After you read this book, re-take the assessment
quiz to see how differently you may feel about
yourself and the prospect of dating in the months
ahead.

1. ___Y___N Do you know what you are
   looking for in a long-term relationship?

2. ___Y___N Are you aware that happiness comes from within and does not depend on a relationship?

3. ___Y___N Are you optimistic that you will find a potential partner?

4. ___Y___N Do you communicate in ways that build trust and increase intimacy?

5. ___Y___N Do you feel confident that you've cleaned out the baggage from your past?

6. ___Y___N Are you open and receptive to making personal changes that would enhance a new relationship?

7. ___Y___N Do you feel comfortable talking about sexual issues on a date?

8. ___Y___N Are you aware of the signs and symptoms of an abusive relationship?

9. ___Y___N Can you bring up difficult issues with your partner easily, knowing it will strengthen and deepen the emotional connection?

10. ___Y___N Do you have the character and qualities you are looking for in a partner?

CHAPTER 1

YOU'RE LOOKING FOR HIM—IS HE LOOKING FOR YOU?

You look across the room, your eyes meet and you smile. He starts walking towards you and your heart pounds with anticipation and excitement. Does it really work that way? It can. But don't get caught up expecting that kind of *Hollywood fairytale experience.*

When you were in your 20s, chances are appearance was the number one factor that attracted you to your partner. But things are vastly different now that you are middle-aged. Your interests have changed and, hopefully, your priorities are more realistic. Of course, appearance is important, but there are other factors that may be even more significant now.

> *Angie and Carl were attracted to each other from the start. He was charming, tall, and fit with a nice head of hair. On their first date, Angie and Carl got into a heated discussion about politics, and Angie was surprised to learn that he had a completely different philosophy than she. While this difference disturbed her, she felt it could be overlooked. However, it soon became a thorn in her side, reaching the point where they would avoid watching the news together because **it would always end in a fight.***

Do you know what you're looking for in a relationship and why? Consider these three factors before you accept a new date.

1. Your *'absolute must-haves'*: these are the necessities you demand before you could consider dating someone. Your list might include qualities like honesty, fidelity, kindness, or similar political/religious affiliation and educational background.

2. Your *'I need to have this, but will consider other options'*: this might

include height, weight, or qualities like generosity and affection.

3. Your *'it would be nice to have this'* wish-list: here's where you would put things that you'd love to have, but it's OK if they are not there.

The only thing that should be fixed and unchanging is your *'absolute must-have'* requirements–and with those you should never waiver.

Let's consider some of the qualities that would fall into these categories and see which ones you can be most flexible with. Otherwise, they should be considered your *must-have* necessities.

#1: Character

Nobody is perfect. We all have some character flaws, but hopefully not the kind that would make us criminals or psychopaths. Basically, your character is a set of behavior traits that define how you act, relate to others and live your life. It is based on learned behavior from childhood and determines your role as a member of society. Character establishes whether you will reach your goals effectively, whether you will obey the laws and rules of society, and whether you are considered by others to possess healthy qualities. A person with a good character is said to be sincere, stable, and understanding.

Good character means you care enough to be trustful and supportive of the other person, as well as encouraging in a non-competitive, accepting way. With good character, you allow others to grow in self-worth and optimism and to be a more productive person because of the relationship. A person with good character keeps commitments and follows through with what they say. If you build a solid foundation with your good character, your credibility will be respected when an issue comes up.

#2: Values

These are the ideas, principles, and beliefs you hold special. Does your partner share the same values as you in terms of spending/saving money, religious/spiritual beliefs, or moral and ethical standards?

Is he opposed to gambling, sexually explicit movies, or cursing? Does he like to attend church regularly and does he practice his faith daily? Are these values something you also consider a priority?

Sharing similar values and interests creates a strong sense of companionship. You are attracted to someone whose principles and ideals are similar to yours. Plus, this common ground makes conversation and activities flow more easily.

#3: Level of Commitment

Love and commitment can mean many different things to many people. Do these words imply the same thing to you and your partner? Be clear about what you are looking for. Are you expecting that both of you are willing to give your full attention to the on-going relationship with the commitment of fidelity, protection, and support? Does he agree? Does love mean commitment to him or does he have more of a "good-time" outlook on the relationship? When you are both on the same page regarding such important issues, it reduces the chance of misunderstanding and pain down the road.

The greater the similarity there is in both of your perceptions about the relationship, the greater the chance for success. Has he been married before? How many times? And how long has he been single? It's nice to know that other people found your partner desirable, but are you one of his many conquests? And, if so, is he on the rebound or ready to become involved again? Be sure there is a mutual understanding when it comes to what you expect of the relationship. Is it marriage or just companionship?

#4: Generosity

How much significance do you place on material possessions and gifts? Are your expectations regarding birthdays and holidays in accord with the value he places on giving and receiving presents? If not, you may be setting yourself up for disappointment and resentment.

Are you looking for someone who is willing to share his physical possessions and personal wealth to make you happy? While you may find financial security a valuable resource for your future together, recognize that his money is his to do with as he wishes. Also, remember that you too should be willing to share your assets in a mutual bond of respect for each other.

Are your expectations regarding generosity realistic? And are you overlooking other qualities that may make for a fulfilling long-term relationship?

#5: Family Roles and Responsibilities

The relationship he has with his family (grown children, siblings, former wife(s), in-laws, and parents) expresses his family values. These relationships will reflect on how he treats you. If he is estranged from them, it could indicate a problem for you in the months or years to come. Can he share these things with you openly and honestly?

If taking care of aging parents is a responsibility and a commitment your partner made, are you appreciative and understanding of his sense of loyalty and compassion? Do you find his devotion attractive? Know that when you are sandwiched between two generations (children and parents) life can seem overwhelming with obligations, and finding balance can be almost impossible. Try to understand the stress and empathize with him. You may experience the same circumstances yourself down the road.

#6: Appearance

There is no doubt that the better you look physically, the more attention you will get. And the same is true for him. Therefore, a person who cares about his appearance and shows good grooming, who wears clean, contemporary clothes, and smells good will be easily approachable. Does he share your desire for personal cleanliness and overall physical upkeep? You will probably want to attract someone with similar personal standards.

#7: Fun and Enjoyment

It's awkward when you tell a joke and your partner doesn't laugh. It is even worse if he doesn't get your sense of humor at all. Be sure your personalities are in sync when it comes to humor and having fun. Can you both enjoy a concert in the park, a hike in the woods, a picnic, visit to the museum, a stroll on the beach, or is he a movies and dinner kind of guy? How important is this to you?

Does he make you laugh? Is he witty and sharp? The possibilities for having fun are endless. And as long as you both are willing to experiment, you can share days and years of mutual enjoyment. Your compatibility will remain strong since you share a zest for life. Laughter and enjoyment are very appealing and make you more attractive to others.

#8: Dependable/Responsible

A healthy person is responsible for his own behavior and actions. He is able to say, "I'm sorry," and be aware of his contribution to the situation. He is able to forgive by letting go of the past, so you can move on to the present. Healthy relationships do not allow grudges or resentments to build. If he feels responsible for what he says and how he says it, that quality is very mature and attractive.

Punctuality shows dependability. It is a common courtesy to be on time. Your time and his are precious and should not be taken for granted. Be respectful of the other person by being where you are supposed to be, at the time designated. Examine if you place a high priority on promptness.

#9: You Can Be Yourself

It is very comforting to know you feel safe expressing yourself. That means your communication is comfortable and not strained. You are able to discuss your need for intimacy and security. You are able to pursue the relationship in an environment that is safe and secure. This relaxed atmosphere lets you be yourself and is a very attractive component of a healthy relationship.

The bottom line is this–if you are looking for someone who has particular qualities that make you feel good and bring out the best in you, then make sure you possess these same qualities yourself. After all, if you are looking for them, someone else is also looking for them in you.

As for Angie and Carl, they are no longer together because of the strong differences in their general philosophy and principles. While Carl physically met her standards, Angie realized that there are more important things to consider before you get seriously involved. She is determined to find someone with whom she can talk comfortably about anything and who will share her same perspectives on issues of importance to her, such as politics or religion.

CHAPTER 2

RELEASING RELATIONSHIP BAGGAGE

All too often, the weight of your past is carried on to your next relationship. When you bring along these old hurts, it's a sure-fire way to sabotage your new love. The bottom line is that no one should enter into a primary relationship with someone who is still carrying their old baggage–and that includes you!

If you are concerned about your own insecurities or have doubts about going into another relationship, acknowledge yourself for your wisdom. It's time to clean out the baggage that's holding you down. This process will open you up to create the kind of healthy, happy relationship you have been looking for and deserve.

> *When Ray found out her husband was having an affair, she was completely devastated. She thought their relationship was sound and loving. She knew she devoted 18 years of her life to being a good wife and mother. However, she did not know what went wrong. Now divorced, she is still trying to get past the pain and trauma of her experience. Since that time, Ray has dated several men. Nevertheless, she's suspicious and untrusting. Ray thinks her apprehensions about her past are sabotaging her new relationships and she's not sure how to break the cycle.*

If you also have unfinished business weighing you down, the following steps can help you complete the process of closure.

#10: Identify Your Feelings about the Past

Your previous relationship may have left you with some unresolved issues and anxiety about your future. Ignoring the situation doesn't work. It always comes back to haunt you. So, it's time to examine your relationships to understand how the past is creating chaos in your current romantic life.

What commonly happens is that your doubts and negative emotions trigger irrational thoughts or behaviors within you. These feelings grow, and instead of being able to let them go, you unconsciously repeat the programming in your next relationship. This causes a cycle of unhealthy behaviors that can ruin any potential for peace and harmony. You must come to a place of realization that giving those negative emotions so much power over you is a waste of time and energy.

You want to be able to pinpoint what's troubling you and identify the underlying problem. Identifying the problem is the first step to releasing it. Notice any patterns that are common in all your relationships. While you may not be at fault for some of these patterns, there may be others you are guilty of perpetuating. Be responsible for changing what you can about yourself. At the same time, it is crucial to realize that it is not your responsibility to change anyone else. This is, of course, a lot easier said than done. However, if you keep that insight in mind, it will help you steer clear of playing the old *'change'* game with a partner who has no interest in modifying his basic behavior.

#11: Feel so You Can Heal

If you feel sad, angry, guilty, bitter, hurt, resentful, or disillusioned, it's best to acknowledge those emotions so you can work on getting past them. Feelings that are suppressed are usually uncovered by some trigger, like a familiar song, a comment, a certain look, a particular restaurant or other place, etc. When you identify your emotions and understand them, the triggers that elicit those emotions are no longer charged. In fact, you feel nothing at all, and that neutrality is good, if you want to move on with a new relationship.

#12: Let Trust Build Slowly

Trust means you have faith that your partner will be honest, keep promises and not abandon you. If someone disappointed you in the past, you may feel jaded about trusting anyone new. To help build trust again, ask yourself how long you want to feel self-defeated and angry? Once you realize that these feelings are no longer useful, you are ready to let them go and move on.

It is important to get to know someone slowly, so that you'll see the true person you are involved with. You may start by sharing some small confidences to see what happens. If the confidence is breached, then move on to your next relationship. If not, you can continue sharing larger, more intimate secrets as you begin to feel comfortable that your partner is trustworthy. People are very complex, social creatures, but without trust, you can never really be close to another person. And closeness is something we all crave and need.

#13: Acknowledge the Lessons as Gifts

Instead of repeating the mistakes you've made over and over again, stop blaming others and begin identifying where you can change. What part did you play in allowing the hurt? Did you lack the confidence to stand up for yourself? Give yourself the opportunity to learn from the experience and even forgive yourself for your part. Try also to forgive yourself for your naivety. Could you have done things differently? Perhaps, but you did the best you could at that time. Now you know better, so don't make the same mistake twice. Insight is the gift we get for learning our lessons.

#14: Don't Have Sex Too Soon

If you're still having trouble moving beyond the hurt from your past, you may want to delay sexual intimacy with a new partner. Too often it just complicates matters. Any time you plan on having sex with someone, you are making an emotional commitment. If you are not ready for that commitment, you should wait before you become physically intimate. Postpone moving to this new level until it feels right emotionally. Your partner, if he really cares, will be okay waiting until you're ready. How long should you wait? Again, this decision depends on your sense of trust, your ability to release the past, and your sense of self-awareness and respect.

#15: Release the Past through Ceremony

Obsession over past incidents, painful memories, or hurtful partners is counterproductive and will not lead to a new healthy partnership. It prevents you from seeing your potential partner for his own merit, since he is always being compared to your past negative experience.

You can, however, release your past through a ceremonial ritual. All it takes is a few minutes of your time and a desire to do the work. Start by writing a letter to the person who hurt you. Do not hold anything back. After you've written your thoughts, feelings, resentments, and painful memories, put the letter in a fire-proof container and burn it. State out loud that you are releasing all the negative feelings and behaviors from this experience—and really feel it!

This exercise is for you only. It is not meant for anyone else to see. However, it is a wonderful form of release since you get rid of a lot of "history" and allow yourself the freedom to experience more joy, love, peace, and self-respect. Just remember, unless you fill the empty spaces you've just cleared out with good thoughts, all the old garbage will return. Be mindful of what you are telling yourself. Use self-affirming statements and other positive self-talk. Start to believe that you can be happy and deserve a healthy relationship.

#16: Get Rid of Your Sense of Failure

Your past relationship(s) may have been in trouble, but it takes two to tango. Let go of your sense of guilt that you could have done more, anger that you were a victim, or self-criticism that you should have known better. Instead, focus on the lessons you may have learned about love and loving. A failed relationship does not make you a failure. Therefore, learn from your past–don't keep reliving it!

#17: Seek Professional Help if You Need It

There are many self-help books on relationships available in bookstores, but if you need more than books can offer, a mental health professional can help you uncover the root of your emotional pain. Even if it is difficult for you to share your feelings with another person, it is very important to find a way to talk about your pain so you can heal. Just knowing that someone understands how you feel helps pave the way for clarity and acceptance.

#18: Visualize Yourself Happy in a New Relationship

You know what you don't want in a partner, but it's more important to know what you do want– focus on that. Have a clear mental image of your desired partner and see yourself happy together. Even more important than seeing is feeling how you will feel in this relationship. The more genuine feeling you can produce around what you want, the more you will attract exactly what you are looking for.

> *Ray decided she needed to get professional help. Her therapist supported her in understanding her insecurities and how she could rebuild her self-confidence and self-esteem. Ray learned that the energy she put toward her anger and bitterness could also be directed to redesigning who she is. Ray is now back in school finishing her degree in teaching.*

> *On the recommendation of her therapist, Ray journals her thoughts daily to keep in touch with any negative emotions she may still be harboring. Ray feels she is ready to start dating again because she is no longer feeling sorry for herself or resentful about her past.*

Releasing old baggage is very liberating. You feel a weight lift off your shoulders setting you free to have a healthy, long-term relationship. The time that you spend working on letting go of the past will make you, and your potential partner, grateful that you took the time to clear your mind, heart and soul to love again.

Chapter 3

PREPARATION– LOOKING & FEELING YOUR BEST

First impressions are lasting impressions. Sure, it's not always fair, but it's the reality we all live with. When you are dating, you are marketing or "selling" yourself as a great person to spend time with. There are always things you can do to spruce up your packaging. It may take some preparation and work, but what in life, that's really worthwhile, doesn't?

Grooming issues top the list of dating turnoffs for both men and women. Look in the mirror before going out in public. Make yourself as attractive as possible. Then smile and get out there with confidence.

Martha put off dating for more than a year after her husband of twenty-eight years passed away. She was overweight. Not pleased with her appearance, she kept putting off doing anything about it. Time passed and Martha started resigning herself to spending the rest of her life alone.

When her recently divorced, long-time friend, Susan, relocated to her city, Martha got the wakeup call she needed. Together Susan and Martha enrolled in a weight-loss program that encouraged a diverse exercise and nutrition program. After two months, Martha started seeing signs of progress that encouraged her to keep up her efforts. After three months she and her good friend both took the plunge into online dating. They even had a couple of double-dates. Best of all, they're having fun, liking who they've become, and are eager to keep up their more fit and confident lifestyles.

Making changes with a buddy always eases the way into new territory. Here are key suggestions for preparing yourself to look and feel your best. Be aware that this will involve more than just makeup, hair, clothing, grooming, and body image. However, it's always smart to start on those areas that you can do something about.

When you feel in control over your life, you give off the energy of someone who knows who they are. And that is very attractive to others.

#19: Exercise, Tone, and Energize

Exercise has been proven to add years to your life. Why fight it? Find an activity you enjoy–or at least a friend or neighbor to share the experience with you–and make a commitment to exercising several times a week.

The key to success is <u>no excuses</u>. Create a routine that becomes an integral part of your life–and stick with it. If you need the discipline of a trainer, get one and cut out other expenses in your life. If you need to lose weight, determine that this is a lifestyle change you are ready to make and again, commit to it. The real battle is all internal.

Think about how wonderful you are going to look and feel as the weeks and months pass. This is a new you being created, by you, for you! Don't sabotage yourself.

In the meantime, dress to compliment your body. Watch your posture. Get a flattering hairstyle and hold yourself with the air of confidence that says, "I'm worthy of your attention." When you believe it, others will believe it too!

#20: Love Who You See in the Mirror

We've mentioned this before and will again, because, if you don't like who and what you see in the mirror, it will be difficult to convey your value to your dating partners. Look around you. Women in relationships are not all tall, slender beauties. What you are aiming for is an attraction factor that has more to do with the kind of energy you emit than the size of the dress you wear.

It's all about feeling and acting confident because you sincerely like yourself. If you are having problems feeling good about yourself as a prospective relationship partner, don't bother moving ahead with dating just yet. Instead take the time to find a counselor you can talk to. Join a support group. Do the inner work to grow your self-esteem; then test the waters on a few dates. You'll be amazed at the difference in your results.

#21: Treat Yourself to a Makeover

Few women wake up every morning as radiant beauties. Every model uses an arsenal of products and tricks to camouflage imperfections and play up their beauty assets. If you haven't updated your look in recent years, or are not aware of the hair and cosmetic secrets that can enhance your appearance, treat yourself to a professional makeover.

You can find resources for this at the cosmetic departments of better stores, at hair salons, day spas, and boutique clothing stores. Some companies, like Mary Kay®, will even let you test and play with makeup products. Let the experts offer suggestions you might not have tried before. Be willing to experiment. Play with makeup color, hair coloring, cuts and styles, accessories, and jewelry. Try different shoe heights, skirt and pant lengths, fabrics, and necklines. Learn what are the most flattering *'looks'* for you and don't get caught up following fads or trends that are not age, height, or weight appropriate.

You'll feel like a million bucks after a good makeover and that's just the thing you need to start your new dating adventures on the right foot.

#22: Handle Medical Issues and Other Challenges

Health issues aren't that important until you have them! Then they take up your time, demand your attention, and zap your energy. If you are dealing with a health challenge and have been putting off medical attention, make that a top priority right now.

If your life is entangled with other complex issues, don't procrastinate any longer. Child-custody matters, alcohol or other addictions, depression, career transitions, relationship conflicts with your children, and other serious distractions will hinder and complicate your dating enjoyment. Take responsibility for areas of your life that have to be cleaned-up with the knowledge that you are paving the road toward a bright and rewarding future with a new mate. Isn't that a goal worth committing to and pursuing?

#23: Invest in a Great Photo

Think about a business that advertises its product using a poor, ineffective visual image. How likely are they to succeed? Online dating sites offer you the opportunity to showcase yourself in your best light. And that begins with an excellent professional photograph.

A flattering photo is an investment in yourself that you will be proud to send because it reflects you at your best. You don't want to use a photograph that's five years old or one your cousin took at your last family reunion. When you scroll through the faces on dating sites, the photographs inevitably play a major influence in your decisions. Don't underestimate their effect on potential dates looking for someone like you!

#24: Practice Conversing on Several Key Topics

Not everyone is a natural conversationalist. But everyone can improve their skills in this area. Practice conversing with your friends and co-workers on a broad range of topics that would be appropriate for first and second dates. Practice handling sensitive issues that might come up, such as a tough medical history, difficult divorce, or death of a child. Get comfortable asking questions that are open-ended so you can avoid yes/no responses. Have some personal anecdotes you can share that provide information about who you are without being too revealing.

By all means, hone your sense of humor. You don't need to tell jokes. However, if you can lighten up on a date you'll both enjoy the time with each other more. Be willing to laugh at yourself regarding some personality quirks and not take yourself too seriously when discussing facets of your life. Most importantly, don't whine, complain, criticize and share all your regrets on those getting-to-know-you dates. This guy is not your therapist or your savior–and I'm pretty sure doesn't want to be either.

#25: Prepare to Be a More Interesting YOU!

If you're not feeling confident that the YOU package you're presenting is as interesting and valuable as it might be, take action before you start dating. Enroll in some classes or courses online, at a local university, or a high school Adult Ed program. Take dance lessons, tennis lessons, voice lessons or whatever rings your bell! Volunteer at a homeless shelter, animal shelter, or other neighborhood activity that builds your character and interests. These are terrific places to find others who have the same interests as you do and are fun to be around.

When you are busy leading your revitalized life, you don't *'need'* a relationship. You're just more likely to attract one, especially a relationship that honors and complements all the qualities that make you YOU!

#26: Know Your Boundaries

Are you willing to kiss, make-out, or have sex on a first date? Can you turn down those invitations without turning off the relationship? When will you be comfortable meeting a date at your home? How will you know your date is worth moving ahead with a second date?

Everyone has different rules about these topics and differing boundaries within their comfort zone. Before you can discuss such delicate topics with a partner, you first need to contemplate all of these and other related issues yourself. Decide what your boundaries are <u>before you start the dating process</u> and you will save yourself much confusion as you proceed. Then, you can sincerely explain your own rules and values with someone new. And you won't have to apologize for yourself or stumble for the right words.

Sincere partners will respect you for sharing your boundaries and values early in the relationship. If there's little compatibility between you on key issues from the start, you will both be happier to just move on to find a better *'fit'*.

#27: Plan to Have Fun and Be a Fun Date

Are you afraid, intimidated or insecure about starting to date again? Work on changing your mindset first. Know that you deserve to have fun and romance in your life. Determine that you will have fun on your dates. This isn't a dental procedure. It's time to relax, enjoy new company, share experiences, and have some new adventures.

Decide in advance that dating will be an enjoyable new addition to your life. Sure, not every date will hit the bull's-eye for you. But you can still enjoy your time and the company. Approach every date as a learning experience. Discover new places you haven't been, observe new personality traits that are different from yours, explore new possibilities available to you that you've never considered before.

In addition, learn to release and let go of some *'rules'* that have been holding you back from enjoying your life. You *can* try bowling, or attend a doo-wop concert or canoeing–even if you've never done that before. Just make fun a priority. If your dating experience isn't gratifying, move on with no regrets. You're one date closer to finding that someone who is more *'right'* for you.

> *Martha has been dating for more than a year now and has met several interesting men. While none can be labeled 'Mr. Right' yet, Martha has come to enjoy the dating process. As her body is becoming more and more to her liking, she is also finding that she has become a woman she really likes. With that attitude, the men she meets treat her well and enjoy her company. Martha is now very confident about her future and knows she is never going to be lonely!*

CHAPTER 4

ENTERING THE "MEET" MARKET

Where can single women over 40 go to meet single men in a safe, non-intimidating environment? There are plenty of places if you know where to look.

Two things to keep in mind: 1) Never go anywhere that makes you feel uncomfortable. 2) Hanging out at the same venues all the time will not get you introduced to new prospects.

But what if you're shy and have been out of circulation for a while? Let your "name card" do the talking for you. If you don't have a business card with your name, phone number and email address, then make one up. If you feel uncomfortable putting too much information on it, just put your first name and email. It's an easy way to let someone get in touch with you again.

> *Patty was married 34 years when she lost her husband and for the past eight years she had no intention of dating again. Now, however, she finally feels she's ready to get 'out there', but she's also very nervous. After all, Patty hasn't been with anyone else for many years. She's understandably confused and somewhat afraid about what to do. She doesn't know where to start, where to look, or even how to act. Patty feels uncomfortable going to clubs and while her friends mean well, she's not ready to go on blind dates.*

The first thing Patty needs to do is get out of the house and get involved in activities that interest her. Here are some suggestions for ideal meeting places that keep you from feeling like you're on display or in a *'meet'* market.

#28: Adult Education Classes/College Courses

Have you ever thought of taking adult education classes—just for fun? These kinds of classes are usually offered at your local public schools in the evening. Culinary classes are fun and a great way to hone your skills in the kitchen. What man wouldn't love a gourmet home-cooked meal on one of your early dates? And you'll be surprised at how many men are interested in learning to cook, as well!

Find your interest and then learn tennis, golf, bridge, pottery, a foreign language, computer skills, poetry, etc. and see how much fun you can have.

Your local college also offers classes that you can audit, which are free to seniors. You just have to wait until enrollment is complete for matriculated students and then take whatever classes are open. You can also enroll in a college course and benefit from a subject that would upgrade your skills and general knowledge. Find a class you feel passionate about, so even if you don't meet the man of your dreams, you will still be meeting people who enjoy what you love. You can even take a course you ordinarily wouldn't choose, just to give yourself the opportunity to broaden your spectrum. There are also workshops, seminars, self-help lectures, and conferences that attract and bring together people who are positive and forward-thinking individuals.

Taking classes is an easy way for adults to meet other adults and to learn something new. In addition, you are meeting others who share your interests.

#29: Join a Gym

Staying fit and active is important if you want to stay young. Join your local gym, community center, or swimming pool where you'll get great exercise and meet other active people who are interested in staying healthy.

Walking, jogging, and using stair machines are excellent ways to ward off age-related illnesses, like high blood pressure and arthritis. While most men don't attend yoga classes, you'll be giving yourself a healthy way to restore balance, improve flexibility, and renew your connection between body/mind/spirit. In addition, it makes you feel healthier, so you'll look healthier. Best of all, the people you meet at the gym are also interested in keeping fit and trim. What better way to repackage yourself for your new encounter with someone special?

#30: Singles Organizations and Specialty Clubs

Many clubs are geared exclusively for singles. There are travel, weekend outdoors, and nature groups, plus numerous other civic clubs that may interest you. Join a Bowling Club, Square Dancing, Movie or Breakfast Club for singles, or you can start your own club where singles can mingle.

Many national organizations can spike your interest and are great places to meet. The Orchid Society, Republican /Democratic Clubs, Swing Dance Groups, Humane Society, Habitat for Humanity, to name a few, are wonderful places to meet like-minded people who may be looking for other interesting people with the same passion.

You can attend sporting events to find available men, but be sure to brush up on your knowledge of the sport or else your intent will be obvious. Also, be sure you want a man passionate about that sport in your life. Don't attract what doesn't interest you.

#31: Religious Groups

If your faith is very important to you and you prefer to meet someone on a similar path, your best bet would be to stay active in your church or synagogue. You can also attend more than one religious service to meet different people, at different times, and even at different locations.

Many religious groups have small committees that cater specifically to singles. They offer numerous programs, including dances, outings, and events geared to helping singles meet. You may also want to volunteer your services to get on these planning committees. While helping a good cause, you are also available to meet another involved member of your affiliation.

#32: Online Dating

A growing number of women are finding that online dating sites are an incredible resource for meeting prospective partners. Thanks to the World Wide Web, at any time of day or night, you can surf the profiles looking for the perfect suitor. Whether he's an animal lover, hobbyist, athlete, musician, or artist, you'll have a broad choice from among thousands of eligible people. These sites are relatively inexpensive to join and you get to know the person slowly, since you are initially communicating through email.

Not everyone on these Internet dating sites, however, is who he appears to be, so you have to be careful. Pictures and profiles often lie, so be aware that the information may not be absolutely true. Nevertheless, many women report that these sites can be a wonderful way to meet a variety of men. Some matching sites also qualify their members and do background checks before approval. That adds another level of security which might be worth looking for.

Always be sure to use caution when meeting. Choose a busy, well-lit restaurant, park, or other public gathering to get acquainted. Some of the more popular sites for singles are matchmaker.com, match.com, Jdate.com for Jewish singles, seniorfriendfinder.com, and datingforseniors.com.

#33: Networking

Let all your friends, relatives and acquaintances know that you are looking for someone special. You never know who knows someone, who knows someone, who will be perfect for you. Attend all the event invitations you get (weddings, movie night, dinner, game night, etc.) because the more you are "out there" the greater your chances of being introduced to someone new.

Be open to fix-ups and blind dates, if you trust the source. Even if you have to kiss a few frogs before finding your prince, in the long run it might all be worth the effort, if you hit the jackpot. Keep a sense of humor about dating. A "let's see" attitude will get you through some of the more awkward experiences and also reward you with some fascinating new finds when you least expect it.

#34: Bookstores or Coffee Shops

Have a cup of coffee, grab a book off the shelf and enjoy an afternoon of reading. You'd be surprised at how many other people have the same idea, with the majority being singles, looking for other intelligent people to meet. Just don't get so absorbed in what you're doing that you miss out on what's happening around you. You want to be available if someone asks you a question or is interested in what you're reading. Keep your attention open and you might meet a very interesting, bright person.

#35: Host Your Own Party

To add a twist to the conventional party, host your own bash and ask everyone who comes to bring a potluck meal and one new person nobody knows to the event. In that way, you are expanding your circle of friends and meeting brand new people who are already given "thumbs up" by your trusted friends and acquaintances.

#36: Cultural Events

If you're looking for someone with cultural interests, go to museums, art galleries, lectures, and theater events. Maybe you're interested in a person who loves sophistication and elegance. You may want to join dinner clubs or wine tasting organizations. Both are great places to meet new friends since the casual, relaxed environment, usually organized by a club or business, encourages people to mingle, and engage in conversation. It doesn't hurt that the alcohol will make it easier to strike up that conversation. Just don't overdo it or you may end up giving the impression that you are a lush.

Charity functions are also a good place to connect with your community and to have a good time. They attract people who are interested in the cause and willing to give of themselves, a quality which makes for a good partner.

The meeting places are definitely out there. Now you have to show up, as well.

A word of caution: be wary of men who sweep you off your feet at your first meeting. This may be a strategy or tactic they've used many times before. Interview the men as you would anybody you are meeting for the first time.

Remember, you can meet someone anywhere, anyplace, at any time or location. The key is to be open and receptive to new people, when they interact with you, so you can be ready no matter what.

Patty finally decided to get out of the house and venture over to the local bookstore to find a particular book that Oprah recommended. Her intent was to sit down to read the first chapter. She ordered a cup of coffee, but there wasn't any Sweet 'n Low®. At the counter, a man graciously offered her his extra packets. They started talking and before she knew it she was having a pleasant chat with a very nice guy–who eventually asked to see her again.

When you least expect it, at the least obvious moments, you may meet your someone special. Be ready for anything.

CHAPTER 5

WILL YOU RATE ON YOUR FIRST DATE?

Let's say you've been in communication with someone who strikes your interest. Most likely you've been talking on the phone to get acquainted. Perhaps it's someone you know through business or other activities and they've asked you out on a date. You might have met him through an online dating service or through a friend. Now it's time to connect, in person, on a first date.

> *Rona and Rick were "set up" by Jason, a mutual friend who knew they both volunteered at a local animal shelter. Jason suggested they meet because they had so much in common. Jason asked Rona if he could pass her phone number along to Rick.*

Trusting his judgment, she agreed. Rick called her up one evening and they chatted for about ten minutes. He asked if he could call again and they spoke for twenty minutes this time. The conversation seemed to flow well.

When Rick asked if Rona would like to get together in person, she agreed to meet him the following Saturday at two o'clock for a cup of coffee at Barnes & Noble. Rona felt comfortable in meeting him because the conversational chemistry so far was good. They did have some strong mutual interests that could be a stepping stone to getting better acquainted. She told Rick she had another appointment later that afternoon, so he knew in advance that she had some time constraints. That gave Rona an opportunity to pick up and leave if things were not moving along well.

Rona was prepared for her first date. Here are some guidelines so that you too can relax and enjoy your first-date experience without regrets.

#37: Psyche Yourself Up for Success

People are attracted to confident, self-assured people. If you approach dating from a place of insecurity and fear that will project to everyone you meet. A healthy woman is not looking for a father-figure or someone to rescue her. She wants a mate, a confidant, a partner, and friend in life. To attract that kind of man you have to come across as a desirable, self-confidant woman. That involves doing the inner work.

If your insecurities are substantial, get private counseling before starting on the road to dating. If what you need is a spirit boost, look yourself in the mirror and acknowledge all your desirable qualities. Then make a list of your many attributes, talents, and positive personality traits. Start believing in yourself and knowing that there is someone out there who will appreciate who you are.

Become aware of your self-talk. Catch yourself putting yourself down, calling yourself fat, boring, stupid, or any other term you may have previously used to make yourself feel less valuable to the world. Start consciously calling yourself "a babe" or "a great catch" and begin visualizing yourself laughing and walking hand-in-hand with someone special. Keep mentally affirming, "I deserve a great man and I'm attracting him into my life" or some other phrase that resonates with you.

Start anticipating success and feeling like the woman you want to be. Know you deserve to share your life and attributes with some other very lucky person–because you found each other!

#38: Have Realistic Expectations

It's not reality, but our expectations about reality, that set us up for pain and disappointment. Write down your expectations about meeting a new partner. Then look at them objectively. Are they realistic? Are you looking for Brad Pitt to fall into your arms thereby making any other guy a lesser choice? Are your demands about age, weight, height, financial success, and other factors limiting your ability to find a high quality partner who will love and appreciate you? Do you imagine yourself buying a wedding dress and planning your reception after every date?

Don't do that to yourself. Prioritize what really matters to you. Be flexible, realistic, objective and fair in your expectations. Then go out and be pleasantly surprised when your "Mr. Right" package enters your life–even if some warts are included.

#39: Dress within Your Comfort Zone

There is something sad and desperate about a woman who doesn't dress her age. We all strive to look stylish and fashionable. We all want to emphasize our assets, through our clothing choices, while playing down our flaws. But when your skirt is too short, your neckline too low, your jewelry is too gaudy, or your hairstyle is too over-the-top, people notice you for reasons you didn't really intend.

When you dress comfortably and appropriately on a date, you don't have to think about your appearance. You can be relaxed and focus your attention on your partner, where it belongs. It's always valuable to check your clothing with a friend first, if you want help in deciding what to wear. You can also get your wardrobe reviewed by someone you respect who dresses well. Do you need to add some contemporary pieces to your closet while throwing away others that are out-dated?

Your goal is to look natural, well-groomed, and elegant in a simple way that reflects you. Most men are looking for someone they feel comfortable bringing home to meet their family and friends. Be that woman!

#40: Prepare Yourself with Questions

Stammering to create conversation can be awkward and a turn-off for both parties. Be prepared ahead of time with several questions you can ask that gets your date talking about himself. Hopefully, you can then interject some information about you, as well, to keep the dialogue flowing.

Talk about current events, your work, hobbies and other activities, favorite vacation spots, sports, interesting movies, or books you've read.

Touch briefly on your children and his as well as your pets. There will be time to learn more about them as you get better acquainted. Avoid discussing divorce, past relationships, the death of your husband and similar subjects. This first date should be light and provide a basic introduction into your lives so that there's interest in learning more.

#41: Be Prepared to Answer Questions

Have some answers prepared in advance, as well, for subjects that may come up about which you don't want to talk in depth at this time.

Be willing to talk about yourself, but don't dominate the conversation. Answer questions in a way that promotes a give and take, making it more conducive to comfortable self-disclosure on both sides.

#42: Choose Comfortable Places to Talk

For a first date suggest meeting during the day, perhaps late morning or afternoon on a weekend. Evenings are more formal date-wise and should be reserved for second or subsequent dates.

Always choose a casual environment. A bookstore, coffee shop, ice cream parlor, or park is a great place to sit and chat without pressure or a lot of noise. Go for a stroll. Avoid expensive restaurants where issues about who pays for the meal can be avoided. Keep the date light-spirited and easy. Make it an appetizer that is so appealing you can't wait for another date, to try the main course.

Wherever you go, make sure it's an environment that is conducive to real conversation. Sitting in a movie theater or attending a play or concert will not give you much opportunity to get to know your date. There's time for those experiences together, once you both feel the connection warrants meeting again.

#43: Minimize the Length of Your Date

Your first date is a test-run for you both. You want to get to know this person enough to determine whether you desire to see him again. Avoid meeting for more than an hour or two the first time around. That should set you both up for planning another date to keep the energy flowing and learn more about one another.

Sometimes couples get so enthralled with each other on the first date they talk endlessly and hate to separate. The next time they see one another, there can be awkwardness, because they have covered so much ground so quickly there is little left to say. Keep the excitement and energy of your new encounter by disclosing more and more on each subsequent date.

Another reason for this approach is to slow down the process before moving into physical intimacy. If you get too close too quickly, sex moves into the picture prematurely and can create an awkward and uncomfortable outcome for a budding relationship that just needed time to unfold.

#44: Be Gracious—Even When You'd Rather Not

It's easy to be enthusiastic, cordial and complimentary when you are pleased with the person sitting across from you. However, it is important to mind your manners and be gracious even if it's a frog you're talking to who you will never date again.

You never know when you will cross paths in the future or who this person knows who may be part of your social network. Smart women remember "this too shall pass," keep their spirits up for the duration of the date, and mind the rules of etiquette. When you treat others as you'd like them to treat you, ultimately you will be rewarded. Who knows, this guy may have a younger brother who is perfect for you!

#45: Don't Discount a Good One

Not every happy and lasting relationship started with love at first sight. Studies have proven that many women marry men who they were not that interested in, at first. That happens to be the case in my own circumstances. It was only after casually dating my husband for a couple of months that I started realizing what a "gem" I really had in my life. He got better looking, more interesting, and more charming the better I got to know him. I might have passed up one of the "great ones" had I moved on too quickly.

So be willing to go out again if there are enough qualities that work for you. Give him a try. However, don't settle for anyone who gives off red flag warning signals. Trust your gut and keep your antenna up at all times.

Rona and Rick picked right up with their conversation when they met on their first date. Both of them loving pets was certainly a strong anchor for their connection, but they had to learn a lot more about one another. Fortunately, Rona liked what she learned about Rick. Talking to him was easy for her and she enjoyed his sense of humor.

At about 3:30, she excused herself to make her next appointment and Rick jumped right in to ask her out again. Next time they're going to dinner on a Tuesday night at a casual eatery in town. Rona's looking forward to their second date and, truth be known, so is Rick!

CHAPTER 6

RELATIONSHIP TRAPS—PITFALLS THAT SNAG

Relationships should be life-enhancing. That's why we're attracted to meet and spend time with other people. In reality, however, too many relationships are not at all what you expected or even close to what you wanted. Let's explore why.

The relationship you have with your partner is special. Your partner is there to grow with you and to share in your life. However, if you expect too much from someone or put too high an expectation on someone else's role, you are setting yourself up for failure. In other words, don't rely on a fantasy to fulfill what you desire.

When Sandy and Stan met, they knew they had a lot in common. Both had grown children, living out-of-state. They both lived in New Jersey and moved to Florida at about the same time. They were both divorced and ready to meet someone new. But that was not the whole story.

When the relationship began, Sandy didn't know that Stan still attended his ex-wife's holiday gatherings. Nor did she know that he supported his youngest son, who is out of work. Sandy soon discovered that he only wants to see her once a week. His reason, he is involved in many activities with male friends. Sandy wants more than just a casual relationship and is easily hurt by his lack of commitment and his inability to "read" what she wants.

Sandy is upset and resentful about expectations she had regarding Stan, ones that he wasn't even aware of. Like so many other boomer women, she set herself up for failure by not paying attention to the pitfalls of unrealistic expectations.

Here are the common relationship mistakes you can avoid. They will help you and your partner not to fall into the resultant trap of disappointment and frustration.

#46: Not "Reading" the Other Person Accurately

You don't want to become too co-dependent or needy. *It is not your partner's job to make you happy.* Of course, it's reasonable to expect to feel happy when you are with your partner. However, it should never become his "responsibility" to boost your mood or please you 24/7.

You also don't want to take responsibility for his feelings or actions. Do not be so overly attached to the outcome of your partner's personal life challenges, that you forget who YOU are or what you are feeling.

Not recognizing the needs of your partner can become a major area of contention in any relationship. In his book, *Men are from Mars, Women are from Venus,* John Gray states that if men and women don't understand each other's needs, it is very difficult to know how to fulfill them. The easiest solution is to discuss what you need from your partner and do this in a clear and concise manner. That means leave nothing to assumptions or guessing.

Women can be vulnerable to "fairy tale" thinking. We assume if our partners really loved us they can also read our minds. This absurd conclusion sets us up for relationship disasters, repeatedly, because it's based on an erroneous assumption. Men cannot read our minds. If something means a lot to you–gifts on Valentine's Day and your sixth month Anniversary, for example–mention that to your partner months in advance. Find out if they have similar feelings. If they feel no nostalgia about celebrating the date you met, realize you are making an unrealistic request that is not likely to be met, especially as the years go by. You then have to decide whether meeting that need is essential in your life, or you can let it go. Focus on the deal-breakers that are meaningful needs for you. Learn about your partner's deal-breakers, as well. Compromise when you can. Discuss areas that need to be straightened out, and let go of expectations that are unlikely to be met. If you don't clarify your true needs from non-essential wants and preferences, you'll be frustrated and disappointed throughout your relationship with your partner.

On the other hand, it is wise to avoid invalidating your partner's needs, feelings, opinions or values by considering them wrong or over-exaggerated. When you say, "I knew that already," you are diminishing your partner's content and shutting them off. Let them finish their thought, without interruption. This way you increase your chances of building trust and respect.

#47: Focusing on the Negative

Successful relationships are built on mutual respect. If you focus on the negative aspects of your partner or the relationship, you will reach a place where you can no longer appreciate the positive. Nobody is perfect, and if you expect him to be just like you, you'll be disappointed. Avoid magnifying your partner's faults so that you deny yourself all the positive, attractive aspects of the relationship you noticed when you first started dating.

It is common to bring up old baggage from the past, but it is not healthy. People who fixate on their past tend to bring a great deal of negative energy to the present. Those who get caught up always planning for the future tend to miss the value, joy, and wonder of the here and now.

Therefore, don't place too much attention on the future or the past as it reduces your ability to enjoy what you currently have.

Develop a clear set of priorities and be willing to let go of minor infringements. Does it really matter that he keeps a picture of his ex (with the kids) on his wall? Who cares if he dated a lot of women as long as today his interest rests entirely on you? Enjoy what you have, because if you start worrying about all the "what ifs…" you'll lose the potential for a healthy, growing relationship.

#48: Avoid Competing

Be careful that you are not competing with your partner by letting your egos, rather than your hearts, run the relationship. Often partners will _react_ to each other instead of choosing to _respond_ to the person behind the behavior. Reacting seldom comes from a place of contemplation or reflection. It can be too abrupt, intense, or anger-based. Responding usually means you have considered the options, and made a decision about how best to express your needs. Positive responses are more likely to lead to other thoughtful responses, therefore, promoting a dialogue, which is what two mature adults want when discussing differences of opinion.

Sometimes, people become addicted to winning. For them, it's a constant personal challenge to come out on top when they fight, cook, play sports, or engage in general banter. "Win" fighters feel this approach adds fire and dimension to the relationship. If you have to keep the relationship alive with competition, it is usually not a healthy situation. Relationships are not a competition, but rather a connection. Neither partner should be made to feel wrong or insignificant in order to boost the ego of the other. Rather, relationships are a give and take that involves sacrifice, compromise, letting go, giving support, and being happy for the other person's successes.

#49: Losing Your Individuality

If you think that intimacy doesn't require individuality, you are wrong. It is not necessary to do everything together or be completely compatible. It is unrealistic to think that you will never want your own space. Many couples suffocate each other by forcing extreme *'closeness'.* In the long run, this *'closeness'* tends to create an unhealthy atmosphere–especially for one of the partners. Overcome your fear of being alone. Allow your partner his alone time. When you are together, you can share what you experienced on your adventures apart from one another.

If you find yourself afraid of being alone, seek out professional counseling and guidance. It is not your partner's responsibility to heal the wounds of your past or compensate for childhood disappointments. It is _your_ responsibility to learn how to love and respect yourself, enjoy time with yourself, and find peace and fulfillment in your autonomy. If you cannot, you will find one relationship after another falling apart. No one can fill or "complete" you. The movies and novels are just plain wrong–and many women just need to "grow up" and grow to love themselves first before they can authentically love another person.

#50: Not Discussing Important Issues

You should never put off or ignore discussing important issues like marriage, sex, religion, and finances. Is your partner financially unstable because of his career choice or because he's paying alimony/child support? These important topics should be openly shared early on in a relationship. Things will not change for him while you're dating, so be aware of how high a level you put financial security in your criteria for a mate. Is he recently divorced and not ready to make another commitment? Or is he enjoying playing the field, with you as one of his playmates? Are you feeling fulfilled sexually–or faking it so as not to wound his fragile ego? Are you comfortable sharing your religious philosophies or practices–or is there conflict every time the subject comes up? Talk about these important issues before you get too emotionally attached.

#51: Avoid Patterns of Criticism

Avoid getting into patterns of criticism, statements of contempt, defensiveness, and withdrawal. This pattern evokes negative responses, which always leads to arguments and resentments. No one can be expected to be criticized continuously and still be open to being a warm and loving partner in return. Put yourself in your partner's shoes when you feel the need to criticize. Use empathy and compassion to guide you.

If you speak when you're angry, you may say something you can't take back. The damage is already done. Take a time out when you are too emotionally "hot" to respond rationally. Then get back to the subject when you can speak without using a barrage of expletives you may later regret.

#52: Not Being Friends First

The basis for a healthy relationship is friendship, and friendship is the catalyst for genuine feelings of love and commitment. It is always a good idea to develop a friendship with your lover first based on the criteria you look for in a friend. Treat each other the way you would treat a close friend. A friend is someone you accept with all their flaws and weaknesses. A friend knows your likes and dislikes and understands why you do what you do. This level of comfort and intimacy translates into a solid foundation for lovers to blossom and grow together.

The relationship should move slowly and progress at a pace that is comfortable and secure for you. Make sure your boundaries are clear, at the onset, to avoid confusion and disappointment. The problem with many relationships is that women become intimate before they actually know who their partner really is.

#53: Playing Games

Do you feel comfortable with yourself? Are you acting a part, doing what's expected, and then stopping after you get to know the person? Nobody enjoys being with someone who is insecure or inauthentic. Therefore, at all costs, avoid playing games. It is one of the fastest ways to ruin your relationship. Be honest, genuine, and realistic. You never want to leave the other person in doubt about what to expect from you. Don't act helpless, stupid, or incapable when you're not. You don't have to play games to convince the other person that you have value or that you care; you just have to be you. If being you is not enough for your partner, why hang around? There's someone more suited to you waiting to be found.

#54: Don't Stop the Romance

Just because you are a couple, it doesn't mean the romance has to end. The early romantic stage of a relationship is sometimes not sustained as the relationship progresses. Spontaneity and surprises should continue throughout the relationship, because they are thoughtful and a special gesture that your partner will always appreciate. Cherish and nurture the relationship and it will be the best investment you ever made. Underestimate your partner and you will sabotage this special gift.

By all means, leave love notes, buy flowers, laugh, and don't take each other for granted. The biggest relationship mistake is making your partner feel insignificant in your life.

Your ability to navigate your relationship requires emotional and intellectual skills and the wherewithal to know that you are responsible for making or breaking the experience. Therefore, if you found a like-minded, eligible individual, who meets your standards for getting involved, don't mess things up by being unwilling to give him significant attention and care.

> *Sandy has been feeling like a second class citizen to Stan and his friends. She did not know some important information about his financial situation and his level of commitment. Sandy now understands that he may not be able to give her what she needs and she is ready to move on to find*

the wonderful, attractive, "enlightened" person she craves.

CHAPTER 7

COMMUNICATE–TO ATTRACT THE RIGHT MATE

By midlife, you have settled into certain behavioral patterns that either support or inhibit a healthy, intimate relationship. Did you know that the most important element of a successful partnership is your effectiveness as a communicator? Good communication should improve your connection, build trust, and enhance intimacy. However, if communication is poor, it can do just the opposite and destroy the foundation that holds a relationship together.

Maggie is a single woman in her early 50s. Her life is lonely as she is desperately looking for Mr. Right. However, she is biding her time by dating someone who is far off course. Her current boyfriend is "overly honest"–a trait that makes him too outspoken in sharing his thoughts and observations. This guy is not aware that his desire to be "frank" is really a way of hiding his anger, insecurities, and confusion about the relationship. Maggie is unable to express her feelings because she's afraid he will criticize her. Neither one of them is really listening when they communicate, or genuinely aware of how the other is feeling.

Remember that every interaction involves two or more individuals–each caught in their own view of the world. Both parties send out opinions, attitudes, judgments, and other messages in an attempt to "share" and create a mutual understanding. However, communication is not just about *what* you say, but *how* you say it.

Here are some of the basic tools for creating effective communication. First, understand and master them yourself. Then, talk to your partner about them and why they are so important in opening the door to—and then maintaining—a healthy and fulfilling relationship.

#55: Emotional Intelligence

Listening is the most important skill you can acquire. When you talk, the listener will generally hear 25 to 50% of what you say. Therefore, when you speak to your partner for 10 minutes, he is really only hearing 2–½ to 5 minutes of the conversation. How can you change that?

Your ability to listen is based on your capacity to understand your emotions and the emotions of your partner. This ability is labeled Emotional Intelligence. The idea of Emotional Intelligence encompasses several principles.

- Are you and your partner able to act considerately in response to each other's feelings?
- Do you both possess the discipline and empathetic capacity to channel your emotions in a healthy manner?
- In other words, are you both objective, insightful, patient, and appropriate in your relating to each other?

How you handle your feelings is a skill that can be learned. It is vital to the harmony you experience with your partner. You will then be operating out of a conscious state of understanding. This allows you to remain open and receptive to other distinct ways of looking at the world. Research supports that people with the highest Emotional Intelligence tend to be the happiest.

#56: Acquire Active Listening Skills

There are specific skills you need to practice to make your listening more effective. Using these techniques will encourage communication. It will take time and seem awkward at first, but once you master these skills, the process will become more natural and effortless.

1. Pay attention to the conversation by nodding, smiling, and encouraging short phrases like, "Is that right?" or "I hear you."
2. Reflect back what you hear by paraphrasing, "So what you're saying is…" and clarify things with questions like, "Is this what you mean…?" You'll be amazed at how often we misinterpret what is being said and need concrete clarification to get the message straight. This is especially common when the

discussion turns to emotionally charged topics which are common as relationships develop.

3. Don't interrupt. Patiently wait your turn to respond, until you've heard the entire point of the message.

4. Never attempt to dismiss, discount, or demean what your partner is saying. It only puts them on the defensive. You gain nothing by attacking the speaker.

5. A good communicator doesn't make or expect their partner to become a mind reader. This can lead to miscommunication where your intent is not understood. Never assume anything, especially that the other person knows what you are thinking or feeling.

6. When you don't like or agree with what's being said, learn this important skill. Start by validating the other person's viewpoint. That means you admit the possibility that their point of view could make sense. You are not agreeing with them directly, but just acknowledging that two different perspectives can both actually be right. This acknowledgement will show your partner

that you have a real interest in problem-solving and fairness.

7. After validating what you heard, it is much easier to state your perspective as another equally valid option. Sometimes two people have to agree to disagree and move on, harmoniously with life. We cannot always convince another person–even one we love–to see the world our way. Learning to accept differences and move on is a sign of maturity. Develop that ability.

#57: You/I Messages

One of the easiest ways to start an argument is by sending a "you" message to someone. What this does is lay blame. Sending a "you" message encourages the receiver to react defensively. Comments like, "You make me so angry!" usually add fire and escalate an argument. The retort can be, "I make *you* angry? What about you? You are so…." and the fight takes off.

Ideally, if you send an "I" message about how you feel about what was said, you may get your message across differently. When you say, "I feel upset when you say that I make you angry and I would like you to be aware of that," you are communicating how you feel and ultimately what you would like to happen. You are communicating in a way that is less intimidating or accusatory.

#58: Share Your Problems/Concerns

In a significant relationship, you want to feel comfortable sharing problems. This ability to share serves to strengthen and deepen the emotional connection. What you want to avoid is an argument in which the goal is to win, above all else. Dr. Phil says that if people try to "win" an argument, the relationship fails.

Try not to be sucked into comments like, *"You sound like my mother,"* since they are meant to bait you. Recognize it for what it is and tune it out.

Also keep in mind that it may take hours, or even days, for a person to sort out all the information being discussed. So, don't have unrealistic expectations that you can resolve every problem right then and there.

#59: Complain Constructively

Complain constructively so that you don't wind up hurting the other person unintentionally. Understand how to handle yourself when your buttons are pushed. Utilize the skills to cool yourself down (breathing and taking time out). Avoid attacking each other in areas that are too sensitive. This could add salt to an already tender wound.

Don't drag up everything from the past if you get into a conflict. Make it a personal rule to stay on the issue. Conversations that bring up old concerns tend to escalate into more explosive arguments and bitterness. You are both coming into the relationship with a lifetime of baggage. Because of that, you may have your buttons pushed by issues from an earlier time unrelated to this relationship. Try to work on your own attitude first, so you can get yourself unstuck and be open to moving on.

Criticism, contempt, defensiveness, passive-aggressive behavior, and withdrawing are all detrimental tactics. You always have a choice. You can either say things that nurture the relationship or you can use words to tear it down.

It's your decision. When you display a lack of understanding about one another's needs you are creating distance. Emotions intensify when a person's dignity is attacked.

Conflict can be positive when it encourages growth and strengthens the connection between two people. Conflict caused by unexpressed expectations creates the opposite result. Unfortunately, these types of conflict are very common and should always be avoided. First, examine yourself. Identify whether your expectations are realistic and shared by your partner. Otherwise, you will continue to experience deep disappointment and frustration.

#60: Understand Nonverbal Cues

Learn to understand the nonverbal cues of the other person, so you can better tune into their undisclosed feelings. Watch for eye contact, facial expression, tone of voice, posture, and intensity of touch. Maintaining good eye contact suggests that the person is interested, sincere, and caring. Touching can be soft and friendly or it can be aggressive and scary. Be aware of the enormity of your own nonverbal messages.

Your nonverbal language continuously sends conscious or unconscious signals to others. Nothing has a greater impact on a relationship than the messages you send that are "wordless." Your body language is vital to keeping your relationship strong and healthy. You may not always know what triggers people, so be aware of how your actions and body language might look from their perspective.

#61: Call a Time Out

When you get angry, it's a good idea to pick a private, quiet place to talk. If you are too angry to talk now, call a time out. But always state where and when you will talk later.

When one person becomes silent or stops talking, it is very frustrating for their partner. Keep in mind the fair-fighting rules that include stating what the problem is and focusing only on the problem. Try to attack the problem, not the person–listen with an open mind.

Be sure to address your issues rather than avoid them. Avoidance allows things to fester. Thus, they morph into a much larger, more damaging argument. Don't make generalizations, like "you always…." or "you never…" These generalizations are usually inaccurate statements that will only increase tension.

How you and your partner handle anger is important. Be aware of the different styles and see where you both fall. Do you suppress your anger and let it boil inside you? Do you take things in, and then let it roll off your back? Are you hot and cold in the same minute? Everyone expresses anger differently, which may be part of the problem in avoiding conflicts.

Ask yourself: "Do I want to be right or happy? Is this argument really so important to me that tomorrow or next week, I'll still be thinking about it?" These questions may help you pick and choose your conflicts and reduce some unnecessary bickering.

#62: Learn to Forgive

Ideally, all conflicts should resolve with forgiveness, appreciation, and gratitude. Statements like, "I am so grateful that you…" or "I thank you for…" are ways to express your intention to keep the relationship open and free of unnecessary resentment.

When you forgive, you are letting yourself move on with a clean slate. You are also releasing yourself of the negative thoughts that linger inside and cause you discomfort and distress.

Remember, forgiveness is not about vindicating another's actions or agreeing with them. You forgive for your well-being–not theirs. Forgiveness means you let go of painful thoughts and feelings that cause <u>you </u>hurt or discomfort. It is an act of personal empowerment, not weakness. Forgiving your partner for errors they made is also healthy. It opens the door to their forgiving you when you are at fault. Since we are all "human", isn't that a good agreement to have in a relationship?

#63: Be the Catalyst for Change

Your partner may not be aware of the many tools available for improving communication. Therefore, you need to be the catalyst to encourage this kind of change. With communication, usually one partner needs to initiate the new style or technique, so that the other person can realize its effectiveness. Therefore, you are the role model. Make it your responsibility to change your style in order to change your circumstances. This effort takes patience, but the outcome is usually very positive and rewarding.

Maggie and her partner have to become more aware of how they address each other. Both need to communicate in a manner that encourages effective listening skills and self-awareness. With greater focus on reading one another's needs, they can understand how their emotional patterns are affecting each other. In that way, they will improve how they relate and learn to share in a way that enhances their relationship.

BONUS TIP: Develop your sense of humor!

A good sense of humor can repair or even mend a conflict by lightening the mood. Humor can show the absurdity or foolishness of a situation, or at least ease the tension between you. Laughter is always good medicine. Don't make a joke at your partner's expense. Instead use self-deprecating humor to show you are "human" and imperfect. When you can joke about your own faults and imperfections, your partner is more likely to soften their stance, get the message, and let go of the defensive, self-righteous tone that fuels discord. Develop the capacity to laugh about your flaws and your relationship will be a lighter, happier experience for you both.

Communication is a two-way process. When one person tries to make changes and the other doesn't, it makes for a very difficult relationship. Hopefully, you and your partner will become aware that conversations are a joint experience. When you experience less emotional stress and negative energy, you will appreciate all the effort and conditioning you put into practicing these new skills.

CHAPTER 8

KNOWING THE WARNING SIGNS OF ABUSE

Sometimes you don't realize it, until it's too late. Some relationships can be insidious. And if you're not careful you can become a victim of abuse.

Every now and then, you meet someone who is crafty or sly and operates in a deceitful manner. Before you know it, you're hooked. You're caught in a web of confusion and anxiety. You're living a life that is riskier than you ever expected.

These relationships always seem to start out like a dream-come-true. When the warning signs appear, as they inevitably do, you're hesitant to rock the boat. You're too involved to question what others can easily see. Look at what happened to Stacey, as she got caught in one of the most dangerous types of relationships:

Stacey is on her third marriage. Her first marriage was brief, but her second marriage lasted ten years and produced two children. However, when she found out her husband cheated on her, they divorced. The divorce was bitter and she was left with little financial security and low self-esteem. She met her third husband, Tom, and had a whirlwind romance, only dating six months before they married. Tom seemed to be everything Stacey had ever wanted. He showered her with gifts and said all the right things.

Today they are married two years and in counseling. Tom is going to therapy with some resistance, stating that she's the one who needs the help. They both complain there is no communication and he has threatened divorce, because he's tired of all the bickering. One day he packed his things and without warning, left, but not before he trashed the garage. Tom doesn't want Stacey talking to her ex-husband during the

*day when he's not around. He does not want
her to speak to her sisters, since they don't
like him. He doesn't want to discuss things,
so he retreats into his "cave" and ignores
her. Tom claims Stacey picks fights all the
time, and he just can't take it anymore.
Stacey claims she just wants to understand
why he is always mad, intimidating, and
irritable.*

This scenario is an example of a classic abusive relationship. It is based on power and control over another person. There are various tactics that the abuser uses to gain this power. Below are some of the signs to be aware of, which should expose major "red flags" for you.

#64: Quick Attachment

Notice if your partner expresses his "undying love" after knowing you for just a short while. Your partner may come on very strong with comments like "I've never felt like this before," or "You are different than anyone else I've ever met." This initial stage in the relationship is considered the "honeymoon phase" where you are showered with gifts, flowers, and he is extremely attentive and charming. Be careful of smooth talkers and "very" charismatic people, as they are charmers who get you emotionally attached before you even know what happened. A realistic romance should progress slowly, with each party giving and taking, as you establish your emotional bond.

#65: Jealousy

Jealousy is not a sign of love. A partner who is excessively possessive or jealous—one who calls you constantly or shows up unexpectedly at work—displays a lack of trust. A jealous person may prevent you from talking to, or making friends with the opposite sex. This jealousy is a clear indication of their insecurities and inadequacies. It is a common tactic used to prevent you from growing into a well-rounded and socially-connected person. Don't be flattered or taken in by jealousy. When expressed in the extreme, it is an emotion that can spell danger in any relationship.

#66: Isolation

Be cautious if your partner tries to cut you off or isolate you from family and friends. Does he make the excuse that he doesn't want to share you with anybody? Does he claim others are "causing trouble" or "don't really love you?" The abuser's insecurity is again revealed when he doesn't want you exposed to the thoughts and opinions of others.

#67: Minimizes Behavior

Abusers rarely accept blame for problems or mistakes. They will usually accuse you of something that went wrong with statements such as, *"You made me get angry,"* or *"I wouldn't have done that if you didn't provoke me."* Often, they have a logical explanation or rationalization to justify their behavior. The excuse usually encompasses a bad day, childhood wounds, or something you did previously. They avoid taking responsibility for their own actions, at all costs. Abusers tend to minimize their behavior while focusing on yours. Blaming others distorts, harms, and destroys the self-esteem of the person being blamed. This blaming causes self-doubt and insecurity.

#68: Quick to Anger

Be wary of partners who have a quick temper. One moment they can be fine–the next they get explosively angry. The only emotions they show are anger and irritation. The abuser appears to find pleasure in making others feel inferior. Be cautious of anyone who gets angry enough to throw things or pound the table. Some may even demonstrate hypersensitive tendencies, becoming easily insulted. They take the slightest comment as a personal attack. Also notice if your partner withdraws or avoids conversations. By "turning off" or giving the silent treatment, the abuser tries to control the relationship. These actions reflect a lack of openness and empathy towards their partner.

Very often an abusive person displays "normal" behavior to the outside world, being pleasant and responsible when with others. In fact, they can be overly generous and kind. This Dr. Jekyll and Mr. Hyde behavior will confuse the victim and keep you engaged in the relationship thinking that he "has changed" or is making an effort. However, it is through sudden and dramatic changes in mood, within the privacy of your home, where their true personality will reveal itself.

#69: Intimidating

Often abusers will flaunt a certain look, tone of voice, or stance that is scary and makes you fearful. You tend to walk on eggshells around them, trying not to get them riled up. They may appear insensitive to the feelings of family and friends and show little empathy when others are in pain or suffering.

#70: Verbal/Sexual Abuse

Frequently, an abuser will make statements that are verbally or emotionally abusive such as, *"You are stupid,"* or *"You're fat."* When you react they are likely to say they are, *"Only kidding."* Abusive partners may threaten to hurt pets, children, or you if you want to end the relationship. They are excellent manipulators and will easily find ways to discredit you or make you feel "crazy" by saying things like, *"You're over-reacting,"* or *"You're just too sensitive."*

An abusive partner may make scary or unrealistic demands on you sexually, which leaves you feeling uncomfortable or inadequate. They show no respect for your desires or feelings and will threaten you with harm if you don't comply. Most often, they don't believe that their "violent" behavior should have negative interpretations. They show little awareness of or guilt for violating their partner's boundaries.

#71: Rigid Role Expectations

Women in abusive relationships often complain that they are expected to be a partner according to the abuser's guidelines i.e., house should be clean even though you work or dinner needs to be on the table at six. Trying to live up to their unrealistic or unspoken standards complicates issues even further, creating a no-win situation, which makes them constantly vulnerable to the abuser's explosions of rage.

It is common that these abusers also have very "traditionalist" values. Their values position them, in terms of their role, as the dominant figure. The woman's role is that of submissiveness and subservience.

#72: Controlling Personality

An abuser likes to drill you, wanting to know what you did and who you did it with. They will often control the finances because they "can do it better". They may demand you dress a certain way or wear your hair the way they prefer. In order to increase their personal power, the abuser has to diminish yours, making you feel weak and unimportant. This person usually does not encourage you to make your own decisions without their advice.

These partners also show a low frustration point and poor impulse control. Their personality is erratic and unpredictable, and they get annoyed easily. Often, they may exhibit road rage or extreme impatience and intolerance. They have a difficult time being fair—especially when they get angry. Abusers are usually unable to appreciate all that you do and will complain that you are not doing enough.

Remember that while you are in your early dating period, both of you are on your best behavior, perhaps guarded. However, some individuals are experts at hiding their true personalities until they have you emotionally attached and vulnerable. They may appear charming and pleasant to people outside, and irritated and unpleasant to those who truly know them. Don't misinterpret the above behaviors as normal conduct, and never as romantic behavior. If you find yourself caught in a relationship like this, there is no shame in asking for help. In fact, it's the best thing you can do. Talk to someone immediately. The important thing is to be aware of what is happening and to stop it from continuing.

> *Stacey is still in counseling, learning to stand up for herself, to be less needy and more autonomous. She is increasing her personal power–including the values, worth, importance, and respect she has for herself. Whether Tom comes to therapy or not, it is important for Stacey to understand what motivates her and drives her intentions to be involved with someone like him.*

Keep in mind that many women believe that with love they can change their partner's behavior, perspectives, or personality. However, this is invalid thinking. No one can change another person unless that person is willing and receptive to making those changes themselves.

Note: For the purposes of this chapter, the abusive partner was male. Eighty percent of reported abuse cases are generally men abusing women. However, women are equally capable of being abusive. Also, it is not uncommon to find abusive relationships among same-sex partners.

CHAPTER 9

BALANCING INTIMACY AND SEXUALITY

Feeling close with another person is something that happens over time and develops through shared experiences and mutual commitment. The closer you are, the more intimate you become. Sometimes that can be startling. After all, this person knows you really well, including all your flaws, quirks, obsessions, and dreams.

Intimacy starts by taking one step at a time and by building levels of familiarity and trust. Many people think of intimacy as the sexual component of a relationship. However, sex is just one part of the whole, which also includes emotional and spiritual compatibility.

Although dating and sex are usually attributed to the younger generation, we know that mature individuals are finding sexuality to still be an important part of their lives and something they are not willing to give up. And why should they?

When Abby met Glenn she had been alone for ten years and dated only occasionally. While married, she led an active and satisfying sex life with her husband, but it's been many years since she's been sexually intimate with anyone. She feels unattractive, with her twenty pound weight gain, and somewhat embarrassed to get undressed in front of another person. She'd like to get closer with Glenn, but the thought of having sex is scary.

Whether you are just exploring your new sexuality as a recent dater, or you've been around the block a few times and not satisfied with the outcomes, this advice will be of value for the future. Here are some common areas to explore to help you get in touch with your true-self and to understand and even celebrate your womanhood.

#73: Understand Your Comfort Zone

Here you are single at midlife, after a divorce or death, and struggling to find a comfortable place for your sexuality. What used to turn you on may not work anymore. If you haven't been with anyone since you lost your long-term partner, you may not feel comfortable letting someone touch you in an intimate manner. This may be the best time to create more intimacy by trusting yourself, your prospective partner, and the process.

On the other hand, you may feel excited and more relaxed about exploring your sexuality at this time in your life. After all, you no longer have to worry about the kids walking in on you, or even getting pregnant. You are able to enjoy, relax, and have fun with your new partner.

In either case, you have to understand what makes you feel most comfortable and not be afraid to explore ways to rejuvenate and revitalize your life inside and outside the bedroom.

#74: Find a Support Group

If you are uncomfortable about your sexuality, seek out a support group to help. In a safe, non-threatening environment, you can discuss your fears, doubts, and insecurities and learn new trends and information you may not be aware of. Just a little education and confidence can make a huge difference in how you feel about yourself and your body. Plus, it's always reassuring to discover that you're not alone.

#75: Expressing Affection

Affection is the glue that holds people together. Couples do better when each partner expresses affection in small amounts, consistently, throughout the relationship. It's not that difficult to express your care and regard for someone by making small gestures. Actions like holding hands, giving hugs, tender touching, or gentle kissing are very meaningful gestures. Leaving notes in secret places is always an exciting way to express how you feel.

What turns you on sensually will also turn you on sexually. The slightest sign of appreciation can go a long way in developing a loving relationship.

Of course, there are always people who may be uneasy giving affection in public, or even articulating how they feel. If you or your partner is like that, realize that relationships are a give and take proposition. Pushing away emotionally can only result in loneliness and resentment.

#76: Talking to Your Partner about Sex

If you have concerns, questions, or doubts and are ready to talk about sex, you may want to practice what you want to say beforehand. You might try writing it down, or talking to a close friend. Also, consider where and when to have this talk. Should it be right before you are going to bed, while you're watching TV, or in a casual situation? Understand how difficult this conversation may be for you, and know how it will be equally as difficult for your partner. However, this is an important discussion and can improve all aspects of your relationship.

Your partner is not a mind reader. Try to share your likes and dislikes, desires, and even fantasies. There are some women who think that they couldn't possibly talk about sex in that way, that it's too embarrassing. If this is the case for you, maybe it's time to step "outside the box" and try a different approach to bring you and your partner closer and more in tuned intimately.

#77: Libidos High and Low

Every woman's sexuality is different and is affected by many factors, including menopause, confidence, self-esteem, and past relationships. Some women will experience a slight decrease in sexual desire, due in part to lower levels of estrogen. Look in the mirror and with some positive affirmations in hand, lovingly state how beautiful and perfect you are. This will improve your self-esteem and even ignite this area of your life, simply by your intent. Recent research has proven hormone supplements, herbal products and gels, to be viable alternatives to improve a woman's sexual response.

Women with strong libidos may find themselves more confident. They enjoy a better body image than younger women, and an even more satisfying sex life. If this describes you, then make the first move and bring the relationship to a whole new level.

Remember, what is pleasurable for one woman may not be pleasurable for another. Therefore, do what makes you feel good, and you will find that you are worth the effort!

#78: Sex and Body Image

A woman often bases her self-image/body-image in large part on how she looks. Unfortunately, many women are very critical of their bodies and assume they are aging poorly. They may feel unattractive because they focus on the extra pounds, grey hairs, and wrinkles. Your partner may see you in an entirely different light and pay little attention to the "flaws" keeping you up at night.

What is most important to realize is that sensuality and desire may change as you age, but it doesn't have to disappear. You can still look for and enjoy intimacy as you always have. It is even healthy for you to do so. Therefore, look beyond what you think will keep someone from finding you attractive. Then, do the inner work to help yourself feel attractive and proud of how you look. Confidence is a turn-on!

#79: Sex, Health, and Happiness

Women over 40 are having sex, but many may not be practicing <u>safe sex</u>. Just because you don't have to worry about getting pregnant, doesn't mean you shouldn't be cautious about catching a Sexually Transmitted Disease (STD) or worse. There is increasing research indicating that mature women are contracting HIV/AIDS twice as fast as young people. Yet, doctors are confusing the symptoms with natural aging (hot flashes, depression, and night sweats) and are not giving treatment until it is too late.

Prevention is the key. Be smart. Talk to your partner about safe sex. <u>Always</u> use a latex condom and <u>always</u> get tested for HIV/AIDS before starting this intimate phase of the relationship. Better to be cautious, than sorry.

#80: Illness and Desire

There is no doubt that chronic illness can damper or even destroy an active sex life. Medication and treatments can definitely affect how you, and your partner, will perform. Arthritis, diabetes, pain, heart disease, cancer, and incontinence can all affect your ability to have sex. Nevertheless, it doesn't have to end it. If you or your partner has a chronic illness, there are several things you can do to improve your sex life. Plan to have sex when you are feeling most energetic and experiencing the least pain. Be sure to talk to your partner about what feels good and what doesn't. Be patient and enjoy the closeness and tenderness of the moment. If you have any concerns, always discuss them with your doctor.

#81: A Satisfying Sex Life

Give yourself permission to enjoy pleasure from your partner. Great sex starts with having a healthy attitude, and by being connected emotionally, both inside and outside of the bedroom. Love-making can be an all day affair. It could start early and continue throughout the day, through signs of affection and endearments. What makes sex satisfying is playfulness. Be spontaneous and creative. Pay attention to each other's needs. Be sensitive to the changes you are both going through. Your sexual health plays an important role in the quality of your life, and happily, even affects longevity.

Sex can be fun at any age. There is no reason at all why it cannot be a joyous and important part of everyone's life.

Abby finally had a conversation with Glenn explaining her apprehension about taking their relationship to a more intimate level.

Fortunately for her, Glenn was supportive and understanding. They decided to proceed slowly and over the next few weeks, Abby was able to regain her confidence and sexual desires. Abby and Glenn now share a loving, close relationship where neither one is afraid to address any concerns that arise.

CHAPTER 10

EMPOWERMENT– ESSENTIAL FOR RELATIONSHIP SUCCESS

Empowerment is one of those words that's often tossed around, but few really understand what it fully entails. Those who have attained a sense of empowerment feel strengthened and enriched in their life. But, until you grasp the essence of what it means to be empowered, it's hard to understand how truly important it is in every woman's life–and why it should become one of your primary goals.

Consider empowerment to be an individual process, a personal path or journey you must take in order to achieve self-fulfillment. Empowerment is a way to increase your ability to make healthy choices. These choices translate into positive outcomes and desired behaviors. When you aren't empowered, it affects your sense of self and your relationships with others. In a new relationship, for instance, a woman may be so willing to please her partner that she forgets who she is and who she can become. This diminishes her self-esteem and prevents her from reaching her full potential, that of an empowered partner in her relationship.

Gail is a 50-year-old divorced, single mom, with two teenage children. Recently she met Roy, also divorced. Gail enjoys being with him and will often cancel appointments with friends if he should call at the last minute for a date. Gail thinks her girlfriends will understand since they know that she is developing a new relationship. Sometimes, Gail feels caught between loyalty to her old friends and responsibility to this new beau. She also feels guilty that she's not being the best mother to her children. She is under a lot of stress because she is trying to please everyone. Gail often gets depressed. She doesn't really know what she wants or how to be happy.

Like so many other women, Gail feels helpless. She feels like her life is out of control. In order to gain back her personal power, she needs to stand up for herself. She needs to gain back her self-respect by re-embracing the issues she deems important. The following are some concepts to consider in order to regain one's sense of autonomy and self-worth–in other words to truly feel empowered.

#82: Learn to Self-Soothe

Take a mental, physical, and emotional break every once in a while to rejuvenate and revitalize yourself. Understand that you always have choices. It's a choice to feel good or to feel bad. It's a choice to feel motivated or to be idle. It is very empowering to know that you can decide *how* you feel, no matter what the circumstances.

Your sense of humor is also a choice. Use humor to relieve your stress. It's important to look at the lighter side of things and to laugh, joke, and be silly. I don't care how old you are; laughter and frivolity will diffuse tensions and help keep you aware of what's really important. Don't take yourself or your situation too seriously. That will only upset your mood and compromise your relationship. Nobody likes to be around moody people.

#83: Discuss Expectations

Be sure to openly discuss expectations before you become too emotionally involved in a relationship. For instance, do you share traditional expectations of the man being the sole provider or do you want to be an equal opportunity provider? Are you the homebody, satisfied to stay inside to read or watch TV while he is the social butterfly, always looking for friends with whom to party? Are you attached to frequently seeing your children and grandchildren, while he has little interest in promoting family togetherness? Differences such as these build up to become major issues if not addressed early on and accepted with grace.

Empowered women understand the value of discussing their expectations to be sure you both have the same intent, values, and goals. When you know where someone is coming from, you will understand the differences and not misinterpret actions or behaviors.

#84: Preserve Your Independence

It is extremely crucial that you preserve your independence in regard to your friendships, personal activities, and interests. As a single person, you've made many acquaintances and connections that you should maintain, even while developing your new relationship. You have your friends and he has his. Keep it that way, and at the same time, develop new friends together.

When you maintain your strong social network of people you trust and who are supportive, you increase your self-worth and confidence. This decision is very important when you are trying to maintain a sense of yourself in the relationship and are striving toward being an equal half of the partnership.

#85: Don't Be a Martyr

Do not be a martyr. Take care of yourself, above all else, to ensure you maintain your health and well-being. You should never feel guilty about focusing on yourself and your personal care. Continuously nurture yourself through your self-talk by repeating approving messages of support and encouragement. Your personal internal dialogue should reflect your belief that you're doing well and deserve the best in life. Say things like, "I am doing and feeling well," "I deserve to be happy," or "I love life and will continue to enjoy myself daily." This dialogue will keep you focused on yourself, something too many women forget to do when in a relationship.

Continue following your daily routine. If eating out often, for example, does not make you feel comfortable (for health or weight reasons), but it is something he prefers, don't sabotage yourself to please him. That is the opposite of empowerment. Consider your health and self-image. No relationship is worth disrupting your life and your well-being. The best thing to do is _be flexible whenever possible, but always maintain the values that are very important to you._

Never compromise yourself for the sake of others. Keep your integrity and the standards that you live by, so you won't feel put upon or diminished by anyone else. Honor yourself by thinking independently and enjoying your own perceptions and opinions. Live authentically, speaking and acting from your own convictions and values.

Eleanor Roosevelt, in her autobiography, once said, *"No one can make you feel inferior, without your consent"* (Klein, 2002). An empowered woman knows that <u>*the most important relationship in your life is with yourself*</u>. To find someone you like is great, but to like yourself is even greater. To respect others with admiration and love is important, but it is more vital to believe in yourself and all the good in life that you deserve. You alone, should be the judge of your own worth.

#86: Know Your Unique Skills and Talents

Recognize your strengths and talents so you can confidently believe in yourself. You are unique. You possess certain qualities that no one else possesses. Know what those traits are. Are you an excellent communicator or writer? Do you love socializing? Are you an avid reader or do puzzles give you the challenge you need? Acknowledge yourself for these special gifts and see them as an enhancement to your relationship. Join a book club, a social networking organization, a Latin dance class, or write your memoirs. These unique qualities are who you are. Whether you are involved with someone or not, you should never forget what you love about yourself. Continue being who you are, so your partner can realize how lucky he is.

#87: Remember Your Four Basic Rights

Always remember you have Rights. You, your partner, and everyone else, all deserve the same things. They are:

1. the right to think what you think
2. the right to feel what you feel
3. the right to want what you want
4. the right to say NO

When you say NO to something that doesn't feel right, you are saying YES to acknowledging yourself and letting in a more loving, supportive experience.

If you have the right to an opinion, so does your partner. That means, through mutual respect and understanding, you can avoid the arguments associated with trying to change someone else's mind.

Your life is yours to control. Work on managing your challenges with skills that help you overcome obstacles and bounce back from adversity. The way you do this is by expecting things to turn out well, by staying calm in the face of turmoil, and by keeping your focus on healthy solutions and actions. When you're in control of your life, you are free to implement the most effective coping skills and management strategies. These decisions will result in better choices and more successful outcomes for you.

#88: Work in Progress

Continue growing and learning from your relationships and experiences. Your depth of character and personality make you who you are, and they are impacted constantly by the deep and meaningful relationships you develop. Therefore, make sure your relationships are based on trust, respect, kindness, caring, and appreciation. In this way, the love you give and the love you receive will only enhance who you are and make you a more interesting and complete person.

#89: Trust Your Intuition

If anything or anyone makes you feel uneasy, don't ignore that sign. It probably is justified. Trust your intuition, which continuously sends you messages and vital information geared to influence your decisions. Your intuition connects you to a greater knowledge that has your best interest at heart. If you start questioning your competency or doubt yourself when you are around your partner, it probably means you should back off. No one should make you feel inadequate or worthless. Heed your internal antenna and move on.

#90: Happiness Comes from Within

Realize that your happiness does not depend on a relationship, but rather comes from within. Happiness is not a destination. You can experience happiness in each and every moment. There is no way to actually *find* happiness. Happiness is a choice we make along the winding road of life. If you keep postponing your happiness, you will lose the ability to appreciate what's right before you. Remember, happiness is a choice–the continual acceptance and enjoyment of what you have, right now.

If she is feeling bad when around her partner more often than feeling good, an empowered woman knows it's time to end that relationship. When she loses her self-esteem, if her partner makes no attempt to help her feel better, it's time to move on. When she starts to remember the good times from past relationships and can only focus on the bad times in this relationship, it's time to say bye-bye.

Gail is learning that what she wants and needs is very important. She is no longer trying to please everyone and is able to share her time between her children, girlfriends, and boyfriend. She understands that she has choices. She has the right to do what pleases her the most. As an empowered woman she knows that's okay. Gail is feeling more secure within herself and is realizing that healthy relationships are all about maintaining a satisfactory balance.

CHAPTER 11

SIGNS YOU'VE FOUND A "KEEPER"

Finding a great relationship can happen immediately for some women. But for most others, you will be dating many men, for many months, before you find "the one". In fact, it may take a while for his true character to be revealed to you. And then, much to your surprise, his laughter, broad smile–even bald spot and love handles–start to become endearing and actually sexy. This means that the good stuff is really great, and that the two of you are headed in the right direction.

When that happens, you are going into this relationship from a position of strength, not insecurity. The past ten chapters have discussed pertinent aspects of most relationships. By gaining awareness about the multi-faceted aspects of a sound relationship, you will become more confident, educated, and selective in choosing a partner. The end result will be a match that you want, feel good about, and know is right for you.

> *Doris (54) and Mike (57) have been dating for six months. They feel compatible on all the important issues and enjoy spending time with each other. Doris loves being with Mike because he is attentive, romantic, affectionate, thoughtful, and enjoys her cats. Mike tells his friends he's found the woman of his dreams and refers to her as his "Sugar Plum." When Doris recently had emergency surgery for appendicitis, Mike was at her bedside every day, cheering her on.*

Doris did indeed find Mr. Right.

If you think you may have found "the one", here are some signs to watch for to be sure you've found a keeper.

#91: You Are Comfortable Being Yourself

When you are with this person you can authentically be who you are and don't have to fake how you feel or what you think. There is no need to push or force things. Everything seems to just flow. You trust that he is who he says he is. You feel happy, relaxed, and safe around him. You have no desire to change any aspect of your partner and you don't have to change any aspect of yourself to be accepted by him.

#92: Time Together Is Enjoyable

You can't wait to share your day and look forward to seeing your honey. You feel like a teenager again. He makes you laugh and be silly. He is invested in the time he spends with you and puts effort into making the dates successful. He goes above and beyond what he needs to do to make you feel special. He remembers little details from previous dates and brings them up again so you know he paid attention and really cares. He surprises you with little gifts or notes of affection and is always ready to compliment you when you're together.

There are no major dramas in the relationship since both of you are honest enough not to play games or engage in relationship bashing.

#93: You're Hooked on More Than Just Romance

You think about him all the time and can't wait to hear from him. You feel you know his heart and mind because you talk and share. He has shown you that he has a lot to offer because he possesses the qualities you admire. He does kind and thoughtful things for you. You find you have many things to talk about and you discuss issues beyond what's going on in your relationship. He reveals his inner thoughts and feelings and you both enjoy sharing these intimate aspects of your lives.

#94: He's Emotionally Available

He shows you he is emotionally intact, by letting you know his hopes and dreams. He is confident in his own skin and does not get jealous if you think George Clooney is a hottie. He shows empathy and genuine sensitivity when your life may be falling apart. He is eager to give support and encouragement, yet doesn't overstep his bounds trying to control or manipulate you. He is not afraid to show his true self, including weaknesses and vulnerabilities.

#95: You've Made a Sincere Best Friend

You are loyal and have no desire to speak badly about him, nor does he of you. While there are some topics on which you don't see eye-to-eye, they are not major and you find little to complain about regarding his character and personality. He shows genuine concern for you and your life. He asks questions beyond your work and children and is truly interested in how your day went. He wants to know your opinions about current events, books, or movies. He's interested in knowing who you really are so he can understand you better. He wants to be around you and is a good listener. He is a reliable source of guidance and support and does not run away when the problem gets too tough.

You, in turn, are equally interested in him in the same way and have a sense that your search is over. You've found a wonderful, if not perfect, match. The chemistry you both felt initially may have lessened, but the connection has deepened. You know each other and like what you see. You stopped analyzing his motives and you've decided he is sincere. You've stopped looking for signs that he's the right one, because you've seen many and are finally satisfied you have found "the one". If you weren't involved with him romantically, you would still be his friend, because he is a genuinely nice guy.

#96: Your Family and Friends Like Him

Everyone values the opinions of their friends and relatives, so this is a critical component of your relationship. If those closest to you approve of your new partner, it is certainly a positive reinforcement that you've made a good choice. If you feel good about introducing him to friends and family, you must be proud of him. You like that he makes the special effort to get to know your friends because he knows how much they mean to you. He also has many of his own meaningful relationships and he has introduced you to them.

You like what you see when he is around service personnel like waiters, janitors, and parking attendants. He treats them with respect and is courteous. This is a great sign that he has good character and will treat you, as well, with respect.

#97: He Keeps His Agreements

When he says he'll pick you up at six, he's on time or will call. He doesn't ditch you at the last minute to pursue other plans. You can trust that he'll be there when you need him. You know he'll be at your side in the doctor's office or your support at the mechanic, if the car needs fixing.

When you disagree or argue–and it is inevitable that you will occasionally–he demonstrates the ability to compromise, making resolution more important than winning the battle. He doesn't like to get caught up in petty disagreements— that shows maturity and some good relationship insights.

#98: There's Synchronicity

You find he shares some similar quirks with you (you both dislike strawberries) or one of your not-so-common interests (you both enjoy the opera). You enhance each other in a way that makes you feel comfortable, not smothered. Basically, you invigorate, not exhaust, each other.

You may share an underlying knowledge of what makes the other person tick. Your relationship seems very natural and appears to connect you on a deeper more emotional level. You may finish his sentences, be calling him at the same time, or experience déjà vu because you are both more conscious of each other's actions and behaviors than with others.

At the same time, he is not clingy or needy. You both continue to pursue your individual interests with other friends without the need to spend constant time together. He doesn't get jealous easily, showing he is self-confident and has no desire to orchestrate your life. You trust him and know the difference between synchronicity and smothering.

#99: You Share a Vision of the Future

When you hear him say, "What should we do this weekend?" you don't cringe. You like the idea that he considers you a couple. You both share a common and unified direction socially and even spiritually. He continues to voice suggestions about how you both can be part of each other's lives. However, he understands your individuality and your need to pursue your own dreams. While marriage may or may not be in the picture, you both can see a long-term relationship as a viable option.

Doris did indeed find Mr. Right. Mike told her he is very happy with the way things are going and gave her a friendship ring to show his devotion. Doris and Mike will continue dating to get to know each other better before making a permanent commitment.

Obviously, when you find your Mr. Right, your attraction goes beyond the physical. You know it takes more than appearance to make a lasting, loving relationship. Ultimately, your partner should be someone who is similar enough to you in crucial areas, such as likes, dislikes, beliefs, background, education, age, and personality, yet have a uniqueness that makes him special. Being able to share life's joys and sorrows with someone else is a key ingredient to your happiness and well-being during adulthood. Why not make your middle years as positive an experience as possible with a meaningful partner who will share the adventure with you?

WORKS CITED

Klein, A. (2002). *Winning Words* (First ed.). Houston, Texas, USA: Portland Publishing House.

APPENDIX:

WORKSHEETS

Notes to Self:

Notes to Self:

Notes to Self:

Notes to Self:

Notes to Self:

ABOUT

AMY SHERMAN

THE

AUTHORS

Amy Sherman, LMHC is a licensed mental health counselor in the state of Florida, with a master's degree in Counseling/Psychology from Vermont College.

She has more than seventeen years of experience in the field and has worked with adolescents, men, women, children, and the elderly. She is an educator, a seminar/workshop leader and a group facilitator, and offers programs and trainings to numerous professional, spiritual and civic organizations.

Amy is also a trained clinical hypnotherapist, specializing in anxiety and health issues. Her passion has always been to empower people so they reach their full potential. She does this by following a holistic approach to therapy, integrating all aspects of the body, mind and spirit into her sessions. She recognizes that the physical, mental, emotional and spiritual dimensions of a person are important for their over-all well-being and that anything is possible with the proper direction. Amy's recent focus has been on baby boomers and, as a boomer herself, she is aware of the special issues boomers face.

Amy is the author of the e-book, <u>Distress-Free Aging: A Boomer's Guide to Creating a Fulfilled and Purposeful Life</u>. She provides ten success strategies and valuable tools that can transform ineffective behavior patterns from the past into a positive perspective based on confidence and high self-esteem. Amy offers individual, family and group sessions in her West Palm Beach office and is available for coaching and consultations by phone. **Contact: (561) 281-2975** or amy@bummedoutboomer.com

Website: Baby Boomers' Network
http://wwww.bummedoutboomer.com

ROSALIND SEDACCA, CCT

Rosalind Sedacca is a Certified Corporate Trainer, an award-winning national speaker, and workshop facilitator. She served five years on the Board of Directors of the Florida Speakers Association and has facilitated workshops for business, professional and spiritual organizations throughout North America.

Recognized as **The Voice of Child-Centered Divorce**, Rosalind is the author of, <u>How Do I Tell the Kids about the Divorce? A Create-a-Storybook™ Guide to Preparing Your Children—with Love!</u> This highly acclaimed eBook provides fill-in-the-blank templates to help parents create an attractive storybook customized with family history and photos to convey, with love and compassion, the six key messages every child needs to hear.

She is also the author of <u>How to Break in as a Professional Speaker or Trainer</u> and is profiled in

Blythe Camenson's VGM Career Portrait book, <u>Writing</u> as well as Dana Cassell's book, <u>Writers at Work</u>.

Rosalind is on the Board of Directors of both WE Magazine for Women and ChildSharing, Inc., is an Expert Advisor at ParentalWisdom.com and numerous other parenting and relationship websites, a Contributing Columnist for MommyMentors.com and a Contributing Author for Exceptional People Magazine. She is also the 2008 National First Place Winner of the Victorious Woman Award and a Distinguished Judge for the annual Mom's Choice Awards.

Today Rosalind shares her expertise through TV and radio programs, print interviews, newsletters, teleseminars, coaching and content-rich articles. To learn more about her Child-Centered Divorce Network, free ezine, and other valuable resources for parents, visit http://www.childcentereddivorce.com.

Additional Titles in The 99 Series®

99 Things You Wish You Knew Before...
Facing Life's Challenges
Filling Out Your Hoops Bracket
Going Into Debt
Going Into Sales
Ignoring the Green Revolution
Landing Your Dream Job
Losing Fat 4 Life
Making It BIG In Media
Marketing On the Internet
Taking Center Stage

99 Things Women Wish They Knew Before...
Dating After 40, 50, and YES, 60!
Getting Behind the Wheel of Their Dream Job
Getting Fit Without Hitting the Gym
Entering the World of Internet Dating
Falling In Love
Hitting Retirement
Starting Their Own Business

99 Things Teens Wish They Knew Before Turning 16

99 Things Parents Wish They Knew Before Having "THE" Talk

99 Things Brides Wish They Knew Before Planning Their Wedding

www.99-Series.com

CPSIA information can be obtained at www.ICGtesting.com
Printed in the USA
BVOW030749260712

296216BV00001B/3/P